THROUGH A CHILD'S EYES

Explaining death, organ donation, cremation, burial and cemeteries to young children using terminology they can understand.

Karen Longstreth

Copyright © 2016 Karen Longstreth

All rights reserved. No part of this publication may be reproduced, stored in a retrieval system, or transmitted, in any form or in any means – by electronic, mechanical, photocopying, recording or otherwise – without prior written permission.

ISBN 13: 978-1537707990
ISBN 10: 153770799X

Contents

Foreword v
Through a Child's Eyes 1
Questions 29
Work Pages 45

Foreword

The idea for this book started several years ago when a mother mentioned she could not find resources to help explain the death of her husband to their 4 year old son. I started writing some of what has evolved and then put the project on the back burner. I am not a trained writer and was not confident that what I had written was good enough.

I have worked with young children for 18 years and can talk to young children in a manner which they can follow. I have tried to take some very harsh and scary topics, death, organ donation, cremation, burial and cemeteries and give some honest, age appropriate explanation as to what these are.

I finally sat down and started, again, my story about siblings Danny and Patricia, their parents and their experience with the death of the children's grandpa. I continued with the question/thought and answer section, listing some of the common questions/thoughts I have listened to, or brought up, in conversations pertaining to explaining these things to children. A friend suggested adding some workbook pages. I think this gives a child or children a place to put, in writing, their memories, what is and was important to them about their loved one and gives them a feeling of importance. That someone is truly concerned about their feelings, about helping them to write down what is important to them so they can always remember their loved one, who has died. That is a scary thought as well, worrying if you will be able to remember your loved one.

As much as possible, allow your child to do their own writing and drawing in this section so it is truly theirs. While what they write or draw may make no sense to you, it will to them. If your child is quite young, you may want to do the writing, making sure you are writing verbatim what they are saying, as lengthy as it may be. This will allow the child to be an active participant in their grief journey.

Thank you to Bob Wilson who provided much needed information in navigating this self publishing process. He spent some time with me giving me information on some great websites to use and answered questions several times when I was overwhelmed with proper formatting. He gave me some positive feedback after reading a bit of what I had written and his suggestion of the workbook pages really adds to the value of this book, giving children a place to record their memories about their loved one.

I worked with Vanessa Maynard, an experienced and talented graphic designer, in designing the front and back cover. Vanessa was patient with my numerous questions. She took the time to get a feel for what my intention was for this book and sent a few renderings that she felt captured my vision. I am extremely pleased with the final design and thank you Vanessa, for all your hard work! I wanted the cover to be hopeful and inviting, not gloomy and sad. Though this topic is not a happy one, I want families to know there can be happiness yet again. We can adjust to our new normal! We must go through the grief to come out on the other side of it with some hope and happiness for the future.

Thank you to Glenn at Sarco Press, who did the interior formatting. After I read about all the necessary do's and don'ts to properly prepare this project to submit for printing, I was quite overwhelmed. I do not have the patience for computers and computer work is not my forte! I prepared my manuscript, then read about the format in which this needed to be prepared, probably not quite the order I should have used. I found some talented designers that could do everything I could not and am very appreciative for their contribution to this project.

You can email questions or comments to Throughachildseyes@aol.com

Through a Child's Eyes

Danny was so excited, today was the last day of school and then, FREEDOM!! Well, at least for the summer. This summer was going to be the best ever. Playing with his buddies, swimming, camping, and best of all, visiting his grandparents. It had been Christmas time when Danny last saw his Grandma Julie and Grandpa Hank. They had come to his house for Christmas but this upcoming summer, Danny and his family were going to go visit his Grandparents home. Danny's older sister, Patricia, was also so excited for this trip. She was finishing up 6th grade and Danny was finishing up 3rd grade.

Grandma Julie and Grandpa Hank lived in the country. While they didn't live on a farm, there was still plenty of open area to play, run and have fun. Danny and Patricia always had so much fun when they went to visit. Nearby neighbors had kids about their age so there were always friends to play with. They played outside all day, almost forgetting to come in for lunch sometimes! Hide and seek, running in the sprinklers, biking, someone even had a real cash register that worked. They would save empty food boxes and then they could play store! There was way too much to do to stay inside all day! Every night they ate dinner with their grandparents and there were always 2 or 3 outings planned each week, picnics, the zoo, swimming at the local pool, the aquarium, baseball games, skating and so much more.

The first few weeks of summer went by quickly. The weather was nice, not too unbearably hot. Danny and his buddies had gotten in many bike rides, trips to the skate park, and some video games. Danny and Patricia did not have to go to summer school this year and while Danny was glad of that, a true break from school, he was wondering why. He did not want to seem to appear too interested in attending summer school so he did not say anything to his mom or dad about it. He figured he would just enjoy the summer even more!

Danny's parents, Don and Emma, had talked in late March. There would be no summer school this year for either of their children because Emma's dad, Hank, had not been feeling well for some time. There had been test after test and finally, a diagnosis that was not promising at all. While praying for the best, they were also preparing for the worst, that Emma's dad would not live for years and years more. They were heartbroken.

They talked to Danny and Patricia about Grandpa Hank and told them he was sick. Since they did not yet know how sick he was there were no extensive explanations about death.

Hank had been a hard worker all his life. As a cross country truck driver, he loaded trucks, drove to his destination then had to unload. Boy, that was back in the day, he thought. Truck drivers now don't do much more than drive the load to the destination. While all that manual labor kept him fit and healthy, sometimes, that is just not enough.

The diagnosis a few months ago put a finality on his life that he certainly had not expected at this point in life. At 68 years old, Hank still thought of himself as a 30 something year old man. Up until recently, he had always felt great and most people were surprised when they found out his age. He was so going to miss his family, not seeing his grandchildren grow up and not seeing his children become grandparents, which was such a great joy. How would they possibly continue on without him?

It was time to place the calls to friends and family. Time was now short and Hank wanted to tell so many people how he felt about them one more time. He hoped he had the time to do all of this. The hardest of all was going to be talking to Danny and Patricia about this. They will be heartbroken, Hank thought. And, their summer will be ruined. Hank clearly remembered the carefree feeling of being in elementary school and the anticipation of that last bell signaling summer break! If only he could survive past summer, Hank thought wistfully. Yet another thing about this illness that was out of Hank's control.

Don and Emma got the call they were dreading at about 7pm one evening. They sat down with Danny and Patricia after they had had their baths for the night. At first the kids could not comprehend what their parents were talking about, surely they were upset about something and not making any sense! How could Grandpa Hank be so sick, much less dying? They just saw him at Christmas time and he looked so young, so strong and fit, this just could not be true!

Just when Danny though things were going from bad to worse, there was even more news that he was trying to figure out. His parents were telling him and Patricia that Grandpa Hank was going to be an organ donor. What in the world was that Danny wondered! He and Patricia had heard things about organ donation on the news, that so many people who were sick could be helped, but gosh, how could that be possible. Danny had no idea how that even worked.

Emma had called the pediatrician's office the following day, seeking advice on how to approach this whole subject of death and organ donation.

The doctor's office was very helpful and Emma had a list of about 10 places to call for booklets and information, as well as numerous websites she could access for some information right away. This was going to be the hardest thing she had ever had to do up until this point in her life, explaining to her children just what death and organ donation were, as well as what happens to someone's body after they die. Then Emma and Don needed to get their children and themselves through this situation, adjusting to their new, normal life. She was so thankful she had her husband Don to help her through this. How were they ever going to get used to this new normal?

Emma and Don sat down with Danny and Patricia the next afternoon. Though the informational pamphlets Emma had called about the day before had not arrived yet , she and Don had spent several hours on the computer the night before. Emma and Don felt a conversation needed to be started. Once the information came in the mail, there would be more conversation and explanation occurring. The conversation started out with telling the kids what was wrong with Grandpa Hank: How did this happen? How come the doctors cannot fix this? How much time is left? After all that the organ donation process was explained. Danny sat wide eyed and listened to his mom and dad. Patricia was also wide eyed and fidgeting with some silly putty.

Don started out, as Emma felt like she was not going to be able to hold a conversation without completely breaking down and sobbing. "Everything that is alive has to eventually die. We never know when this is going to happen. Sometimes people and animals get very old and their bodies just do not work anymore, everything wears out and they die. Sometimes there are accidents that happen and people die and sometimes people get sick. A lot of the time when people get sick, their body can heal and they feel better. Or they may need to go to the doctor.

"Doctors do all that they can using medicine and surgery, to help people heal and get better but sometimes, that is not enough. Grandpa Hank found out after Christmas that he has some tumors growing in his body. The doctors have done some surgery but the tumors are still continuing to grow. The doctors have also tried several medications but they are just not working."

Danny and Patricia sat there, still wide eyed, not believing what they were hearing. They both had so many questions, but at the same time could not think of a single question. How could this be! They had never known anyone who died but they did know a few kids at school who had a relative die or a family friend die. None of the kids ever talked about it so Danny and Patricia still didn't really know what to expect. When Grandpa Hank was visiting at Christmas, he looked fine!

Emma felt more composed now that Don had started the conversation so she continued, "So often when people die, there are many parts of their body that can still work very well. When a person dies, there are no brain waves. A person's brain has to work because that is the part of your body that tells all the other parts of your body how to work. Sometimes, everyone in the family feels like the person who is dying will get better soon. Some parts of their bodies can still be working, like their eyes, lungs, liver and many other parts. Doctors do many, many tests to see if a person's brain is working.

"If someone has no brain waves and the doctors are very, very sure that the person will never wake up, never be able to breathe without the help of machines, then the doctors can often keep that persons heart working to pump blood. A persons heart has to keep beating and pumping blood through the body to keep all the other parts of the body that can still work, alive and working well."

Emma paused, choosing her words carefully, "The doctors can do some surgery and remove the parts, the organs, that can be used for someone else. These doctors are called the transplant team.

They are different than the doctors that work in the hospital helping sick people."

Emma continued, "There are always other people who are very sick and will die without surgery and a replacement organ. For example, maybe there is a woman who's lungs do not work well, she has been very sick for a long, long time. There is no other medicine she can take and nothing more the doctors can do to make her better. The only thing that will help is for the woman to get new lungs. The only way to get new lungs is from someone who is an organ donor."

After a slight pause and a few questions from her children, Emma continued, "People choose to be an organ donor before they get very sick. When you choose to be an organ donor, you are choosing to let the doctors use your organs for someone who needs them. When people tell family members that they want to be an organ donor, they usually have written this information down and they also usually have a sticker on their drivers license that says they are an organ donor.

"First, doctors check for a list of people needing transplants, new organs. They look close to the hospital where the person is dying because it is easiest if they are close to who needs the donated organs. Organs can survive outside the body for different amounts of time depending on which organ is being used. If there is not a person in need close by then they search a little farther away."

Don continued, "After a person who is an organ donor has died, the doctors are given permission to do surgery to remove the organs that are needed. People who need the organs have to do some testing to make sure of their blood type and other things. If there is a donated organ that would be a good match for someone in need, then doctors can do surgery. The donated organ also has to be tested for blood type, other illnesses and several other things.

"So for the woman who needs new lungs, she can go into surgery to have her lungs removed and a machine will breathe for her while the doctors are removing her lungs. Other doctors are busy with the person who died, removing their lungs, and the doctors will make sure these new lungs make it to the hospital where the woman is having surgery getting ready for the new lungs. Sometimes, one person who has died can help many, many people with things like eyes, lungs, heart, kidney's and so many other organs. It is possible to help 10, 20 even 40 other people!"

While this was so much information to try and understand, Danny and Patricia understood quite a bit of it. They would certainly have questions after it had all sunk in and they thought about it for a while. They did know right away that Grandpa

Hank was doing something so wonderful! Helping so many people, even though he would not be here anymore. Grandpa Hank was always trying to help other people and animals who needed help, so they knew he must be very happy to be an organ donor. But right now, even knowing how glad Grandpa Hank would be about that, neither Danny or Patricia felt very happy. They hoped they would feel better about this after some time has passed.

Emma and Don both took a deep breath in and exhaled slowly. Wow they thought! They both could not believe they had gotten through this conversation! Now, to keep moving forward. Of course, Danny and Patricia had many questions and their parents gave each of them time to ask everything they wanted to know or did not understand. Emma and Don were very calm and gentle in answering their children's questions, praying and hoping the whole time that they were saying the right thing and that their children would understand what they were explaining to them. On the inside, Emma and Don were scared that they would not be able to get through this!

Don and Emma kept the answers simple in order for their children to understand, knowing that Patricia, being older, would be able to understand more. They could talk to Patricia alone later if she had more questions. And they knew that as their children got older, there would be more questions, which they could answer in more detail as they were ready for more information. Of course, with computers and the ability to get any information immediately, Don and Emma figured they might need to be ready with more information and answers quickly!

By the end of the week, Danny's whole family was on a plane to go and visit Grandma Julie and Grandpa Hank. Danny was so worried, how would his grandpa look? How would he feel? Would he know them? Could he walk? Could he talk? Could he eat? So many things were running through his mind about his grandpa. Would Danny remember his grandpa, his smile, his laugh, the color of his eyes, the feel of his hand holding his…..if only this was a regular summer Danny thought.

Danny was not sure who he should talk to about these things that were bothering him. Even though his mom and dad told him he could talk to them about anything, he noticed they were very much trying to be brave about everything. He could hear them at night, after he was in bed and not able to get to sleep very quickly. His parents talked about everything and how worried they were. Danny did not want to make things worse. Since they first found out that Grandpa Hank was sick, Danny sometimes talked to Patricia about it but she didn't have all the answers either. He would just wait for some time to pass. Maybe he could talk to Grandma Julie. She was always so helpful and answered all his questions.

When their plane landed, Don and Emma rented a car and the family began the drive to Grandpa Hank and Grandma Julie's house. Emma had let Danny use her cell phone to call his grandma and grandpa to let them know when they were about 10 minutes away. They finally arrived at Grandma Julie and Grandpa Hank's house. Everything outside looked the same, nothing looked different... maybe, just maybe this is going to be a normal summer after all, Danny hoped. He was so excited but nervous to see his Grandpa Hank.

Grandma Julie and Grandpa Hank had been keeping watch out the window for everyone and had been counting down the minutes since Danny had called. They were just making their way onto the front porch as everyone was getting out of the rental car. Wow, Danny thought, Grandpa Hank looks a little skinny and tired but looked much better than Danny expected. Hmmm, Danny asked Patricia "Do you think the doctors are right? Grandpa Hank looks pretty good." Patricia agreed but also said they would have to wait and see how their grandpa felt.

The next month was spent going for walks, going for ice cream, lunch and dinner out a time or two, even a trip to the zoo with Grandpa

Hank riding in a wheel chair so he didn't get too tired. There were also long conversations about everything going on and conversations about past summers and Christmases, so everyone could remember some good times. Emma remembered the time when Grandpa Hank blew his straw paper off his straw, only to have the paper land in the mashed potatoes and gravy of the man at the next table. Danny and Patricia thought that was such a funny story to remember.

Grandpa Hank did his best to explain to Danny and Patricia, "Even though I have been pretty healthy for so many years, exercising and trying to eat right most of the time, sometimes a person's body just does not work the way it should. I have a tumor growing inside me. When you have a tumor, the parts of your body that tell other parts of your body how to work are not working so well. These parts are telling some areas in my body to grow when they should not be growing. There is what is called a mass, or tumor. Tumors happen when some part of a person's body is growing when it is not supposed to grow. The doctors have given me medicine and have done surgery to take the tumor out, but my body is still telling the tumor to grow. Now there are no more medicines that will help my body tell the tumor to stop growing.

"When the tumor gets bigger, it will press on other parts of my body and these parts will have a hard time working. My heart has to work so I have blood pumping through my body. Blood provides oxygen and everything in our bodies need oxygen to keep working. My lungs have to be able to breathe to keep my body alive. When the tumor gets too big, parts of my body that need to work for me to stay alive will not be able to work. After some time, though no one knows how long, these parts of my body will just not be able to work and I will die."

"But Grandpa Hank! What does that mean?" cried Danny and Patricia. Grandpa Hank spoke slowly and carefully, "It means" he said "that I will not be here anymore, not with your grandma, not here to see you get bigger, not here to see and talk to you and your mom and dad. But I believe in God. I have tried my best to be a good person, to do what is right, to help others when I can, and to believe, trust and love God. I believe that there is a heaven and that in a long, long, long time we will see each other again, when you are very, very old.

"Even thought I am not here where you can see me, I will be with you ALWAYS! In your heart, in your memories of all the things we have done together and talked about. I know there will always be things to remind you of me. When you see something that is purple, my favorite color, I know you will think of me! When you hear a silly song we have sung together, I know you will think of me! When you think about the story of me blowing the straw paper that landed in mashed potatoes and gravy, you will think of me. When you smell chocolate cake, my FAVORITE, I know you will think of me!"

Grandpa Hank went on, "I also want you to understand that just because someone dies, they do not want to die! They do not want to be away from their families and the people they love, they just have no choice. People who die, love their families very much and will miss them so much. It will be much harder for the people that are still alive because they will miss the person who died very much. It will be hard not being able to see me anymore or talk to me on the phone. That will take some time to get used to.

"Always remember that the person who died wants their families to be okay, to be happy, have fun, have a good life and not always be sad. I know you will be very sad for a while after I die and I know it may take a lot of time, but the best thing you can do is to always do your best, even when it is so very hard. Do good to honor those who have died. I have lived a good, happy, long life. I don't want you to be sad for so long that you are always sad. I don't want you to be stuck in feeling sad for a long time. You are young, you have so much to look forward to, I want you to be HAPPY! It is not disrespectful or uncaring for you to laugh, have fun or be happy. I want all these things for you!"

Danny went to bed that night with so many thoughts swimming around in his brain! His brain could hardly think but at the same time his brain would not stop thinking, so he could get to sleep! How do you never talk to someone again? How do you never see someone again? How do you always remember someone? Danny had so many questions he was asking himself, that he prayed for a long time that he could do all these things. When it was very late, he finally fell asleep.

The next few weeks went by and Danny and Patricia could see that Grandpa Hank was getting more skinny, more tired and could do less and less. Before long, the whole family gathered around Grandpa Hank after yet another doctor visit. Grandpa Hank and Grandma Julie said it would not be long now. Grandpa Hank's body was starting to shut down, more parts were not working well and other parts would soon not work at all. Within a few days Grandpa Hank was in the hospital.

Everyone spent as much time as they could talking and sitting with Grandpa Hank. Grandpa Hank slept most of the time now and he had a very hard time swallowing. Soon he was just drinking some water and clear soup and not much of either.

One morning, when Danny and Patricia got to

the hospital, they were very nervous when they saw so many people in the hallway in front of Grandpa Hank's room. Standing close together were Don, Emma, Grandma Julie, and three doctors they did not know. Dread washed over them and they knew something terrible had happened. Mom, dad and grandma were crying and hugging. The doctors were talking to them quietly.

A nurse came over to Danny and Patricia and had them sit down on chairs. The nurse sat on a chair in front of them and gave them each a stuffed animal, a brown bear with a purple shirt for Danny and a purple bunny for Patricia. The nurse explained to the kids that in the night Grandpa Hank had gone into a coma. He looked like he was asleep but his body was beginning to stop working, his body was shutting down.

A machine was turned on to keep his heart pumping blood and many tests were done assuring Emma, Don and Grandma Julie that there were no brain waves. All the doctors said that he was not going to wake up, his brain was no longer working. As hard as it was hearing this, they felt a little better when the nurse also told them that now he was not in pain anymore and he was not tired anymore.

Everything felt like it was going so quickly but moving in slow motion. There was so much going on. The doctors were able to do surgery to remove many organs so other sick people could be helped. Someone got Grandpa Hank's heart, his lungs, his eyes, his kidneys and several other organs.

Danny tried to think of good things. Maybe in heaven Grandpa Hank could have all the ice cream and chocolate cake he could eat and now he could eat a bunch since he was not in pain anymore. Looking at the brown bear with the purple shirt made Danny think of his grandpa and right now he really missed him! "Please brain" Danny said, "let me remember Grandpa Hank for a long, long time!"

Later that day, after everyone tried eating dinner, of which no one was able to eat much, Grandma Julie had everyone sit down in the family room. "Oh no", thought Danny, "what is going on now?" Grandma Julie started to talk about things like a funeral , being cremated, buried....what was all this about Danny wondered?

"Grandma, what are you telling us? I don't understand", said Danny. Now it was Grandma Julie taking a deep breath...

"Grandpa Hank has died", she said. "When someone dies, it means that their body does not work anymore. They cannot breathe, walk, talk, eat, they cannot do anything. It looks like they are sleeping, but they are not sleeping. When people die, we have to do something with their body. Now, it is just their body left here with us, because

I think their soul and spirit leave their body to go to heaven. So we have to decide what to do next.

"Often when people are sick, they talk about this with someone they love and they make decisions together about what to do. Your Grandpa Hank and I have been talking about this since just before Easter, soon after the doctors told your Grandpa Hank he was sick. Your Grandpa Hank did not want all of us to have to try and figure out what to do. He knew we would all be sad because we miss him and that maybe our brains would be too slow to think about all of this! If we could think about all of this, he worried that we would have so many choices to make, and it would be so hard. He thought we would spend so much time trying to figure out what we thought HE would want us to do, so he had me write it all down, just so I wouldn't forget."

Grandma Julie said, "There are 2 choices when someone dies. They can be buried or they can be cremated. Being buried means the body of the person who died is taken to a mortuary. A mortuary is a place where people work with respect and love, preparing the bodies of people who have died, so our loved ones can be buried or cremated.

"Kind of like getting a bath, the people at the mortuary are very respectful, and they get the body all nice and clean and dressed in nice clothes. Either the person who died had picked out some clothes they liked before they got really sick, or someone in the family picks out some clothes that they know the person who died really liked. Grandpa Hank picked out his favorite suit and a bright purple striped tie. We took the suit to the cleaners after he wore the suit for Easter. It is clean and ironed and has been hanging in the closet.

"If a person who died is going to be buried, then a casket has to be chosen. A casket is a big wooden thing that kind of looks like a rectangle box. It is so soft and cozy inside with soft fabric and a cozy pillow. After the body of the person who has died is clean and dressed, the body is laid in the casket. When the day comes for the funeral, the casket can either be open or closed. Sometimes families want the casket open so everyone coming to the funeral can see the person they loved so much one more time. Some families want the casket closed but may have a beautiful picture of the person near the casket."

Grandma Julie continued, "A funeral is sometimes in a church, sometimes not. If it is in a church, there is a ceremony, some songs, some praying and some time for family and friends to talk about the person who died. If it isn't in a church, it could happen in a similar way too. After the funeral a special car called a hearse takes the casket to the cemetery.

"A cemetery is where the casket is placed and

buried. Any time friends and family want to visit, they can. In a spot which had been picked out, usually long before the person died, a big hole is dug with a little bulldozer the day before the funeral. When the funeral takes place the next day there is a short ceremony. When the ceremony is finished, the casket is lowered into the ground. After everyone leaves, someone drives the bulldozer and carefully and with love puts the dirt back over the casket and fills up the hole, to bury the casket. This is called a grave. Families usually order a headstone for the grave, where the casket is buried. A headstone has writing on it telling whoever reads it the person's name, when they were born and when they died. Sometimes there is a short sentence or even something funny written on the headstone."

Grandma Julie answered questions from everyone and when there were no more questions, she continued. "Being cremated is a lot different than being buried. Being cremated means you also go to the mortuary. The people who work there get the body of the person who has died, ready. The person who has died is taken to a place where there are very big ovens. The workers get the oven ready and the person who has died is placed lovingly in a special container. The container is put into the oven and after a while, the container is taken out. Just the bones are left. The bones are crushed up into a powder, called ashes, and lovingly placed in a bag, which is closed and put into a box. Even though this sounds very scary, the person who died does not feel this because their body does not work anymore. All the people who work at the mortuary are very careful and respectful when they are getting someone ready to be buried or cremated.

"A family member picks up the box of ashes and they take them home. Sometimes people keep the ashes in a fancy container at home. Maybe they eventually take them to the cemetery and put them in a niche. If they are going to place the ashes in a niche at the cemetery, they can put the ashes into an urn, which is a fancy container, and then the urn is put into a niche.

"A niche may look like a big wall that is divided into squares and each square can be opened. The urn of ashes is put inside a square. The niche is closed after the urn is placed inside. Only the workers at the cemetery can open the niche. Some niches look like rocks and are in the garden area of a cemetery. The family can order a beautiful plaque which has the person's name on it, and maybe their birth date and death date. This can be attached to the niche so whoever wants to visit can find the right niche for their loved one they are visiting."

Wow, Danny thought, this is such a long

explanation. Sometimes things are so complicated, he thought! Grandma Julie continued, "Sometimes the person who died wanted to be cremated and then have their ashes taken to their favorite place and scattered. Some people want their ashes scattered in the ocean or the mountains or somewhere they really loved to be or visit. Lots of times, people keep the ashes at home and put them in an urn or maybe a beautiful vase with a cover on top, or a glass heart container, lots of different things can be used.

"Your Grandpa Hank wanted to be cremated. Earlier today, after the doctors did the surgery to remove all of Grandpa Hank's organs that they could use for other people, the hearse from the mortuary came and took Grandpa Hank to the mortuary. They will get Grandpa Hank ready for cremation and next week we can go pick up the ashes. Grandpa Hank picked out a beautiful black box with purple swirls and dots. We will put the ashes into that box. Grandpa Hank said that if you want some of the ashes to keep, we can go shopping for something that you like, something that can close and even maybe lock so you don't lose the ashes."

Danny and Patricia asked some questions and then discussed what they should buy to put Grandpa Hank's ashes in. They thought of a few stores where they could go shopping after they came up with a few ideas for containers. Patricia had her heart set on a crystal heart container and Danny was thinking about trying to find something with purple stripes.

Grandma Julie continued, "In about 2 weeks we will have a memorial service at church. This is pretty similar to a funeral. We will need some pictures of your Grandpa Hank, so in the next few days we can look through our photos and pick some out together. Then we will have some large photos printed. We can also decide what else to do, do we want some flowers or other decorations? Sometimes, people make donations to a special place the person who died, loved. We can decide and let people know. There will be songs too, so we can pick some songs out together.

"At the memorial service, friends and family can get up and talk about Grandpa Hank. After the service is over, we will come back to my house for lunch and visiting. Maybe we can put together a special memory book with lots of empty pages so people can write down something they remember about Grandpa Hank or write about a funny thing they remember Grandpa Hank doing. Danny and Patricia, why don't you work on the first pages and write or draw some things you think are important to remember about Grandpa Hank? When we are really sad we can read and look at the memory book and remember how special Grandpa Hank was and we can see how many people loved him and miss him by reading what they wrote and drew."

Grandma Julie took a deep breath and leaned back on the couch and closed her eyes for a minute. That was so much to explain she thought to herself, I hope I explained it well enough for Danny and Patricia to understand.

Don added, "Having a special memory book will help us remember we are not alone. Lots of people have had someone they love die, but most of the time, no one wants to talk about the person who died because talking about it may make other people feel sad. We can share the memory book with people who come to visit and it will help make talking about Grandpa Hank a little easier."

Danny and Patricia were excited…well…. as excited as they could be with Grandpa Hank just dying. They were going to be starting off the memory book, helping pick out songs and photos and helping to decide on other things for the memorial service. Then they were going to find beautiful containers for some of Grandpa Hank's ashes. They were a little surprised that they were going to be included in all these special decisions.

Don and Emma wanted to make sure their children were included. After all, they were part of Grandpa Hank's family. Don and Emma also felt that giving their children these responsibilities would help ease a bit of their grief since they were being included to decide some of these important decisions. Everyone helping decide what to do for the funeral would give each person a personal and special memory, making this a little less sad of an event.

The next few weeks were a blur of things to do. Picking out photos and songs, putting together a memory book for people to write in and getting some pictures made. Several of the pictures that were picked out were going to be printed as very large photos and Danny hoped he could take one home with him and find a special place in his house to put it. That would really help his whole family remember what Grandpa Hank looked like!

The memorial service was beautiful. While there was a lot of crying, there was also much joy and laughter amongst people talking about funny things they did with Grandpa Hank. And... so many people wore PURPLE! Grandpa Hank would have loved seeing this, thought Danny!

After the service they went to the cemetery where the urn was placed in a niche, which was part of a big wall. Grandma Julie had picked out and ordered a plaque for the niche but it would be about a month before it was ready. She promised to take a picture of the plaque once it was attached to the front of the niche and send the photo to Danny and his family.

After they were done at the cemetery everyone went to Grandma Julie's house for some lunch. And of course, there was a huge chocolate cake!

Danny's family returned home a few weeks after the memorial service. It was almost time for school to start. This summer has been anything but fun, thought Danny. As sad as it was, Danny was very glad he had gotten to spend some time with his grandpa before he died. Grandma Julie wanted to make sure they would always remember Grandpa Hank. Now Danny and Patricia needed to find a special place to put the big picture of Grandpa Hank that they brought home.....somewhere where they could see him often and remember all the good, fun things they did with him, and to smell the chocolate cake just thinking about him!

Questions

1. How much do I tell my child?

   Answer their question/questions honestly, giving them enough information to answer their question(s). Children will ask more as time goes by and as they are ready for more information and are able to understand more.

2. Do I tell them that the person who has died is asleep or that we lost them?

   NO! They are not asleep and you do not want a child to be afraid to go to sleep. They will interpret this information literally and may then be afraid to sleep, feeling like the same thing, death, will happen to them. Also, telling them that you lost the person who died will send them looking to find that person, literally! As the child gets older and you are giving them safety information such as, if you are lost, find a store worker or a policeman or policewoman to help you, they may immediately go back to the explanation they were given about the person who died, as being lost. They will think, since they are lost, no one will ever find them, they will never see anyone again and oh my gosh! Where will I be going since the loved one who died was never seen again? Use the word died, as harsh, horrible and scary sounding as it may be. And, using correct terms early on, will, in the long run, create a bit more comfort, for your child, in using these terms in conversation.

3. Burial, cremation, this is all so scary sounding, what do I say?

You always want to be honest, using terms and enough age appropriate information as needed to answer their questions. If you come up with some untruthful explanation about cremation, or anything else for that matter, years later, when the truth is learned, which it will be, there could then be trust issues that arise due to the truth not being told originally. I had a conversation about a cemetery , burial and cremation in the car with my children when they were around 12, 8 and 7. We were going somewhere and passed by a cemetery. One of my children asked what that was so I gave a brief, age appropriate explanation, they asked a few questions and we were on to another conversation. When I told someone about this they were surprised that I explained cremation to the my children. I replied that I had to give truthful information since they would only become more knowledgeable as they got older. You certainly do not want trust issues later, children not trusting you because you gave them a made up answer, especially about a topic so important and pertaining to the death of a loved one or friend.

4. Will young children remember everything we talk about regarding the death or illness of someone?

Sometimes when a person, maybe a family member, is sick but the death occurs quite sometime later (cancer diagnosis in which a person may survive even years) young children may not remember everything you have ever talked about. You can be very honest and age appropriate about the illness a person has and even telling them this person may eventually die. Children do not dissect every situation like adults do. Do not be caught off guard, if the death occurs several years later, that the child is surprised and acts like they are hearing this news for the first time. This is overwhelming for adults to handle and sometimes muddle through so imagine a child having to work through all this!

My husband had a brain tumor and choose to leave the family. Our children lived with me. In late August 2002, my daughter who was 12, asked if she and her brothers would be able to go to their dad's house for Christmas. She was shocked when I told her he probably would not be alive by Christmas, he died in Sept. 2002. My husband and I had always been honest with our children about the seriousness of his illness. After leaving the family, we did not get any updates on my husband's health. I was also told I was being negative if I stated my husband would not survive, which was the prognosis from the doctors. While staying positive, one must also prepare for what may occur, which may not be survival. Trying to prepare children for the death of a loved one is not easy, especially if family members or friends are saying you are being negative in doing so. While hoping and praying for the best outcome, one must still prepare for the worst outcome, especially in helping your children prepare!

5. How should I handle school?

   It would be very helpful at the start of each new school year to send in a private letter to the new teacher, even years later, explaining what death has occurred in your child's life and how they have been affected by it. Ask the teacher to be on the lookout for changes in behavior, concentration, etc. This will give you another set of eyes to keep an eye on your child. My daughter was in 6th grade when her dad died and a few years later, in 7th or 8th grade, one of my daughter's teachers talked to my daughter about also having gone through the same experience of having her dad die when she was young. This conversation would not have happened when it did had I not written a letter to the teacher at the beginning of the school year. My daughter was extremely consoled and felt so much better just knowing that, here is this adult in her life, something similar happened to her, and she has made it through!

6. My child feels like they are the only one who has had a family member die, they feel alone.

   No one wants to talk about having a family member or a friend die so everyone feels like no one else has ever experienced this. Also, everyone is sometimes so focused on their own life situation that sometimes it is hard to remember that others are also experiencing maybe a similar situation. Sometimes it is also hard to remember that someone has had a devastating loss of a loved one when they are acting fine, handling it well, don't seem sad all the time. I told my oldest son that if they had all the kids meet in the auditorium at school and then asked for a show of hands of those who had experienced the death of a loved one or friend, there would be many kids raising their hands!

7. No one wants to mention the name of the person who died because they think it will make us too sad. Do we talk about them, not talk about them, how do we let others know what we want?

Remember, even those of us who have experienced a death, still do not know the right thing to say to someone. Different people react in very different manners to something you may say. One person may take great comfort in hearing "I am so sorry to hear about the death of ----- but at least they are at peace now, nothing hurts, they are whole again." Another person may be completely outraged by this comment. Sometimes just a shoulder to lean on and an ear to listen is what is needed at that moment.

If talking about your loved one is something that you would like, tell people that you want to talk about the person who died, have their name mentioned, celebrate birthdays and anniversaries even though they are not here anymore. And while it may make you sad, it will only be for a little while and it would give you such joy to know that someone else was thinking about that person. Many people just want to know that other people still remember the person who died. Make sure your children know that they can talk about the loved one who died. Make sure they know you may be sad or upset talking about your loved one, but you will not be sad or upset for a long time. Also, allowing your children to see you upset, sad or crying shows your child that it is okay to cry and feel upset. Your child may then feel more comfortable with coming to you, talking about your loved one who has died, knowing the sadness will pass. They will also feel more comfortable and safe in expressing their emotions as well, not feeling that they need to hide their feelings, acting like nothing is bothering them.

8. How can we honor and remember our loved one who has died?

   Write on and send up balloons. Go to a place your loved one enjoyed and take the balloons with you. Write messages on the balloons and let them go and watch them until you cannot see them. Have a birthday cake on their birthday. Make something they really loved to eat, or buy it, and sit down and talk about them while you eat. Donate something that would be meaningful to your loved one, donations to a charity, an animal shelter, books to a library, items for a homeless shelter. Know that your loved one would not want you to be sad, angry or hurting forever more. They want you to be happy and they know you will be sad and grieving for a while but they do not want that to be forever.

9. My child won't speak about the death of our loved one, should I be concerned?

   Everyone is different, just as some adults are comfortable with talking about someone who has died, some are not. Kids vary as well. Of course you want to monitor and be aware of changes in behavior. Was the child always more of a quiet person or has that been a dramatic difference since the death of your loved one? Kids may also feel more comfortable talking to their friends or another adult, family friend, relative or teacher. If so, be aware of who these people are that your child opens up to and follow up with them. While conversations should remain confidential, providing a safe arena for the child to feel comfortable in continuing conversation, let this confidant know you appreciate what they are doing for your child and to let you know if anything alarming is going on. Of course, letting a parent or guardian know if a child is talking about self harming or harming others is a must and does not violate the confidential relationship.

10. My sibling died when I was young. I feel like everyone loved him/her more than me. Everyone always talks about how good, how perfect they were. I don't think I will ever measure up.

Remember, no one is perfect nor was perfect before they died. We remember all the good things about our loved one so easily, the good times we had with our loved one who has died. Please remember that the family members who are here, alive, they need not only to be taken care of (young children) but all children as well as other family members need to feel loved, cherished, wanted, good and worthy. Please do not figuratively put the deceased person on a pedestal. Constantly praising them will lead to those still here to feel like they will never measure up, feeling defeated, like it isn't worth trying in any situation.

11. One of my parents died when I was younger. My surviving parent had a hard time taking care of them self much less taking care of the surviving kids. I sure had to do a lot to raise my younger siblings.

As hard as it may be to get up each day and function, attend to daily needs and necessities, you may have to push yourself to do so. Grieving is different for everyone, both in the way one grieves as well as the length of time one grieves. If you feel you are at the point of not being able to function, barely taking care of yourself and you have a family to take care of, a visit to your doctor would be a good place to start. Short term medication may be necessary, counseling may be beneficial and seeking out a grief support group would be greatly beneficial to the whole family. Ultimately it is not a child's place to take care of and raise siblings and run the household. Imaging how overwhelming it would be for a child to not only be muddling through their grief journey but also at the same time have to take care of siblings, cook, keep the house clean, etc. This may seem so overwhelming at first, attending to daily needs of the family, but time will help. It will take some time to adjust to the new normal.

12. Change your route/ routine (mental route too).

In high school my oldest son told me about a student who would harass him. I asked when he saw the student, they had one class together then he saw the student at lunch time when on the way to his next class. I told my son to distance himself from the student in class and then to find a new route to his class so he would not see/walk by the student, removing the opportunity for the student to harass my son. So my son altered his route to class from then on.

Sometimes we need to change our route, physical and mental. When we spend so much time thinking, mulling over a situation, we put ourselves, mentally, in a not so good frame of mind. If the situation is the death of our loved one, we are going to go deeper and deeper into our grief. While this may be what we need to do at first, long term we are not moving forward in a positive manner. Changing our mental route may include changing our physical route as well. Get up and shower. Then a few days later add in getting dressed. Add something else new every few days or every week.

Allow everyone the time to grieve. Everyone is different and remember they are not you! Everyone is on their own time frame, children too. It is up to you to monitor your children and respect their own personal way they are dealing with grief, always keeping safety in mind. Young children may need help in moving forward in a positive manner.

Once time has passed and you feel as if you and your children are moving forward in a positive manner, volunteer somewhere. It is amazing how beneficial it is to focus on others and help others. We are always so in tune with our own situation. It took me a long time to realize that the people I saw in different situations, grocery shopping, at the mall, just out and about in whatever I was doing, they all have stories! Everyone has something going on. It may not be a death of a loved one, but it may be something, for that person, that is just as important.

When we focus on others we in turn experience healing, peace, comfort, compassion towards others, and we are moving ourselves forward in a positive manner. You may also find, though you feel that your own situation is horrible, many times there others going through a much worse situation then we ourselves are.

13. I feel that I should give my child(ren) everything they want because they have lost a parent or a loved one. That was not fair to them and I want them to be happy again. I think they should be able to do whatever they want to do and have whatever they want.

Please do not think that just because your child has to deal with a death of a loved one that they should be able to have whatever they want and do whatever they want. As the old saying goes, life isn't fair. Life happens, we must help our children navigate circumstances that are beyond our control. We still need to teach our children that there are rules in life, at school, at home, at work, in society. We also need to teach our children that they must earn what they want, whether through doing chores or having a job. Regardless of circumstances, they still need to be held accountable for responsibilities, helping others and keeping up with school work.

This may seem difficult at first but consider the alternative. If a child has gone through years of being allowed to have whatever they want or to do whatever they want to do, what is that child facing in the future at age 18, 21, 30? How will they be prepared for life's rules, society's rules, rules in the workplace? We need to provide the tools to get them there when they are young. It would be such a disservice to our children to not prepare them for the future. We want them to be as successful as possible and well equipped!

14. When we told the children about the death of-------- they asked a few questions then wanted to get up and play. That took me by surprise, how could they do that?

Children do not dissect situation as adults do. They do not think " well if x happened then y would happen next then z." They take time to digest information based on what they are ready to work through. When they are ready for more, they will ask. They may mull it over a bit and then move on to playing, reading or some other activity. This does not mean that they are not affected by what has happened or that they do not think about what has happened.

15. How old should a child be to come to a funeral or memorial service.

It depends upon the maturity of the child and the ability of the child to participate in a respectful manner. Most people probably do not want young kids running around being loud. If a child is young, but able to sit quietly then they should be at the service.

I read an autobiography about a famous person several years ago. This took place in the early 1950's. The famous person was a child at the time and their mother died. The mother was taken to the hospital in the morning and had died, never returning home. The famous child had gone to school, never being told the mother was even sick.

I still to this day wonder how that affected the child as they grew up. How could the dad or other family members not tell the children that the mother was sick, much less so critically? We must be honest with our children, giving them age appropriate information. They will ask for more information when ready. Our children are incredibly smart. Let's not do them a disservice in any situation.

Work Pages

Spend some time with your children working on the following things. There are 2 sets of these prompts. If you have more than one child or if you want to do this activity now and again in the future utilize the 2 sets. You may also want make copies of these pages first and work on this again after some time has passed and compare what your child(ren) has(have) written. Are they progressing and moving forward in a positive manner or are they stuck? Are the things they are writing appropriate? Do you see a pattern of self harm or thoughts of harming others? Do they seem to be moving in a positive direction?

Karen Longstreth

What are some important things to include in making a memory book for your loved one who has died?

Karen Longstreth

What color were your loved ones eyes? Can you draw them?

What color was their hair? Can you draw a picture of them ? Or do you have a picture of them you can put here?

Karen Longstreth

What was their favorite color? Can you draw something they really liked in their favorite color?

What was their favorite food? Can you draw their favorite food?

Did they have a pet? Can you draw them with their pet?

Write down 3 places you remember going with your loved one and what you liked most about each of these places and what you did together.

Karen Longstreth

What songs remind you of your loved one who died and why?

Do these songs make you feel sad or happy? Why?

Karen Longstreth

After months or years have passed, how do these songs make you feel now?

Do you like to talk about your loved one who has died? Why or why not?

Karen Longstreth

After months or years have passed do you like to talk about your loved one who has died? Why or why not?

What are some things we can do to honor our loved one who has died?

Karen Longstreth

What do you miss most about your loved one?

Do certain smells remind you of your loved one?

Karen Longstreth

What did your loved one like to do? Did they like sports? Cooking? Camping? Art? Reading? Riding bikes? Can you draw a picture of you and your loved one doing something together?

Can you write a letter to your loved one? It can be about anything, how much you miss them, what you liked doing with them, how you celebrate their birthday now, whatever comes to mind.

Continue your letter to your loved one on this page.

What are some important things to include in making a memory book for your loved one who has died?

Karen Longstreth

What color were your loved ones eyes? Can you draw them?

What color was their hair? Can you draw a picture of them ? Or do you have a picture of them you can put here?

Karen Longstreth

What was their favorite color? Can you draw something they really liked in their favorite color?

Through A Child's Eyes

What was their favorite food? Can you draw their favorite food?

Did they have a pet? Can you draw them with their pet?

Karen Longstreth

Write down 3 places you remember going with your loved one and what you liked most about each of these places and what you did together.

What songs remind you of your loved one who died and why?

Karen Longstreth

Do these songs make you feel sad or happy? Why?

After months or years have passed, how do these songs make you feel now?

Karen Longstreth

Do you like to talk about your loved one who has died? Why or why not?

After months or years have passed do you like to talk about your loved one who has died? Why or why not?

Karen Longstreth

What are some things we can do to honor our loved one who has died?

What do you miss most about your loved one?

Karen Longstreth

Do certain smells remind you of your loved one?

What did your loved one like to do? Did they like sports? Cooking? Camping? Art? Reading? Riding bikes? Can you draw a picture of you and your loved one doing something together?

Karen Longstreth

Can you write a letter to your loved one? It can be about anything, how much you miss them, what you liked doing with them, how you celebrate their birthday now, whatever comes to mind.

Continue your letter to your loved one on this page.

Printed in Great Britain
by Amazon